CONTENTS

TWELVE BROTHERS

*It's easy for brothers to become enemies. What does it take
to become friends?*

Benjamin had ten older brothers. Half-brothers, actually. They
were all quite nice to him – although they did keep forgetting
he wasn't a baby anymore. And probably Judah was the kindest.

"I think you're my best brother," Benjamin told Judah,
"because you're the most fun. To me, anyway.

6

BIBLE STORIES
FOR BOYS

Retold by Peter Martin
Illustrated by Simona Bursi

LION
CHILDREN'S

TO FLORA S.B.

Text by Peter Martin
Illustrations copyright © 2014 Simona Bursi
This edition copyright © 2014 Lion Hudson

Published by Lion Children's Books
an imprint of
Lion Hudson plc
Wilkinson House, Jordan Hill Road,
Oxford OX2 8DR, England
www.lionhudson.com/lionchildrens

ISBN 978 0 7459 6370 9

First edition 2014

Acknowledgments
Bible extracts are taken or adapted from the Good News Bible published by the Bible Societies and
HarperCollins Publishers, © American Bible Society 1994, used with permission.

A catalogue record for this book is available from the British Library

Printed and bound in China, November 2013, LH06

"Dad always tells me to think about Joseph. But I was little when he died. I hardly remember him. I don't really count him any more.

"Do you think it was a lion that killed him? Or a bear."

Judah sunk his head in his hands. "I don't know," he said. "I have awful memories of the day we lost him."

"Lion or bear?" persisted Benjamin.

"I DON'T KNOW!" Judah shouted. Sometimes he wondered if Benjamin liked to drive him mad with the same pestering question.

"Sorry," said Benjamin. "But you can't be sad for ever. Or you'll be like Dad, always moping and going on about me and Joseph being the sons of his dear darling Rachel."

Being the only surviving son of his father Jacob's dear darling wife Rachel was Benjamin's bugbear. He wasn't allowed to do all kinds of things in case he got hurt.

Not long after the conversation with Judah came another thing he wasn't allowed to do: travel to Egypt to buy grain.

Benjamin watched as his ten brothers set off. "Hurry back," he said. "Remember how hungry we'll all be if you don't buy enough food."

The harvests had failed several years in a row. Food was scarce.

Benjamin watched every day for his brothers' return. For nearly a month. At last he saw them.

"Dad! Here they come," he shouted.

Jacob rushed to greet his sons. "Ah! Good news! You're safe!" he cried. Then his face fell.

"Who's missing? It's Simeon, isn't it. Where's Simeon?"

"He was asked to… er… stay behind," explained Reuben. "The Egyptian who sold us the grain thought we were spies. He wants proof of our story.

"Simeon will be allowed home if Benjamin comes to prove that we told the truth about ourselves."

Jacob slumped. "I lost Joseph," he said. "Now Simeon's a hostage. I can't let Benjamin go into danger. I'll die of grief."

"We'll have to go," said Reuben. "There's something else we have to return for anyway. The Egyptian slaves put our payment back in our grain sacks. I'll take the best ever care of Benjamin."

Jacob said no. But still the sky refused to rain, still the crops refused to grow. In time the family had no food left.

"Now we really do have to go back to Egypt and take Benjamin," said Judah firmly. "I'll keep him from every danger. Promise. On my life."

In the end, Jacob agreed. Judah and Reuben exchanged knowing looks as Benjamin excitedly set out with them.

All the brothers except Benjamin knew what had really happened to Joseph. He'd been a boastful, brattish brother. They'd sold him to slave traders. They had made up the story about him being killed by wild animals – the story that Benjamin clung on to. What they had done had been wrong; a ghastly mistake. They felt really, really bad about what they had done and the lies they had told.

Keeping Benjamin perfectly safe was the only way of showing

how sorry they were.

Back in Egypt, the Egyptian who sold the grain gave them a surprising welcome. There must have been a real mix-up with the money the time before because the payment clerk said he'd received it, he told them. Simeon was brought out of jail and he looked positively well fed. The Egyptian asked after the family, their old dad, and so forth. They were even invited to a feast.

Not long after, it was time to collect the grain, load it on the donkeys, and go. The eleven brothers had not gone far when a servant came racing after them.

"There's a problem," he said. "A special silver goblet has gone missing. My master thinks you've stolen it. I have orders to check your grain sacks."

The search began. Ten brothers were in the clear. *It could not have been worse*: the goblet was in Benjamin's sack.

"We will take him as a slave," roared the servant. "The rest of you – get lost. Scoundrels."

In spite of threats, the brothers didn't go. They

followed the servants as Benjamin was taken back to Egypt. They went to face the official who could order the most severe punishment and did not flinch. Judah stepped forward.

"Sir," he said, "my father had two sons born to his beloved wife Rachel. The elder, Joseph, is dead. He was killed by – I don't know, a lion or a bear. Young Benjamin is the other. He means more to my father than any of us do. We cannot let Benjamin stay. We cannot let my father suffer. Take me as your slave instead."

The high official glared. Then, to everyone's surprise, he burst into tears. When he recovered enough to speak he simply said this: "I am Joseph.

"I know you're sorry for what you did. God kept me safe. And now I can help you all. Hurry – fetch my father. You must all come and live here in Egypt."

And the twelve brothers were family again.

THE RELUCTANT SOLDIER

THE STORY OF GIDEON

"Some are born great, some achieve greatness, and some have greatness thrust upon them."* Here is a pleasing story for natural-born cowards.

G IDEON LAY IN a ditch. He cowered as probably hundreds of camels leaped over it.

This wasn't Gideon's regular hobby: he was simply hiding from Midianite raiders. Time and again they rode in on camels to steal

*SHAKESPEARE

livestock and harvest crops. Usually he heard of the danger in time to make it to his secret cave. Today he'd been caught up in the crowd of villagers rushing to safety. A farmer with huge fists had simply lifted him out of his way and dropped him by the side of the road. By the time he'd got his breath back, all he could do was roll into the long grass.

Some time after the last camel had kicked mud over him, Gideon went back to a low-walled wine press. He had been using it as a secret place to thresh the barley. The Midianites still hadn't found it.

He picked up his flail and began beating the ears of grain from the stalks. Working soothed his frayed nerves. Then he had a bad feeling.

Was someone watching him? He felt his flesh crawl with fear.

There he was: a stranger, sitting under a nearby oak tree.

"God is with you, brave and mighty man!" called the stranger.

"Oh, is that what you think?" replied Gideon, with a tinge of sarcasm. "Actually, that God seems to be strangely absent these days, unlike those thieving Midianites."

The stranger narrowed his eyes. "Gideon: I am sending you to rescue your people from them. I will be with you."

Gideon was startled and annoyed.

"Oh, you speak for God, do you?" he said. "Prove it. I'll bring you an offering of food and see what kind of god you are!"

He fetched bread and meat, as instructed, laid them on a stone, and poured broth over them.

The stranger reached out his stick. A tongue of flame leaped from it and burned everything up.

Gideon was open mouthed with fear. *The stranger had godlike power.*

"Don't be afraid," said the man. "I'm sending you on a mission. Wait for your instructions."

That night, God told Gideon this:

"Part one of the mission: stop your people bowing down to ugly idols of false gods. Tell them that they are to worship me alone."

What was Gideon to do? If he obeyed God, he would be public enemy number one. If he didn't... ooh, remember the stranger and the miraculous flame.

He made a compromise plan: he would tear down the idols at night, in secret.

When the people discovered the damage, they were furious.

A local farmer with huge fists took the lead: "Anyone with a shred of evidence, speak now," he demanded, glowering. "Let's get all the details and see who hasn't got an alibi."

The finding out didn't take long.

"GIDEON!" roared the farmer. "Let's get him, lads."

13

As the mob surged toward him, Gideon's father stepped forward. "Don't kill my boy!" he pleaded. "If any god is angry about what's happened to some little statue out here in the country, let the god punish him."

Surprisingly, the farmer with the huge fists seemed to agree. "Come away, boys," he ordered the mob. "Let's see what our god is made of."

The crowd grumbled but they'd lost their zeal for a fight. They watched the skies for a thunderbolt or two. Nothing happened.

Then God spoke again.

"Gideon: it's time for part two of the mission. Summon an army to defeat the Midianites."

For a few short days, Gideon saw himself as a hero. He sent out a call for valiant volunteers. A huge army gathered.

Then Gideon panicked.

"Please God," he prayed. "I'm not used to all this responsibility. I need a sign, something obvious.

"I'm going to leave a fleece on the ground overnight. If you want me to do battle with those murdering Midianites, please let me find the ground dry and the wool covered with dew."

He went to sleep hopeful of having found a way out of trouble. He awoke to find a lump of sopping wool on parched grass. Oh dear.

"And to be really, truly sure," he prayed, "tonight let the ground be wet and the fleece dry."

That's what happened. So Gideon had no choice really. He led his army to meet the enemy.

God spoke again. "You have too many fighters, Gideon. I want people to know that I am the one who brings victory. Tell anyone who is afraid of fighting to go home."

Twenty-two thousand men took up the offer. Ten thousand stayed.

"That's still too many," said God. "Here's a test. Take them to the spring to get a drink of water. Some will lie down to lap it up. Send them home. Others will scoop handfuls, staying alert for signs of the enemy. Choose them."

Gideon was left with three hundred men.

"Now for the third and final part of the mission," said God. "Each of your fighters must take a trumpet, a blazing torch, and a clay jar to hide the flame.

"They must spread out on the hillside all around the enemy camp and wait for night.

"When it is dark, they must listen for your trumpet call. Then each must blow their trumpet, smash their jar, and hold the flame high."

Gideon's men took their places. The stars wheeled across the sky. In the Midianite camp there was an uneasy calm. They hadn't seen much by way of an attacking army, and yet…

Out of the darkness came an eerie wailing. The hillside
lit up with flame. How many attackers were out there, shrieking
their blood-curdling threat? "A sword for the Lord and Gideon."

In a panic, the raiding army fought one another as they
desperately ran for home.

When the warriors returned triumphant and victorious, the
farmer with the huge fists led the cheering. He poked Gideon
playfully in the ribs, nearly winding him. "I'd trust a soldier more
than some ugly old god any day," he teased.

Gideon took a deep breath. "I just think you have to be very
careful which God to trust," he replied.

16

CHOOSE YOUR WEAPONS

THE STORY OF DAVID AND GOLIATH

David was a shepherd boy with a sling and a bagful of pebbles.
Goliath was a Philistine soldier with bronze armour and iron weapons:
what you might call "cutting-edge technology".

DAVID LOWERED A large basket to the ground in front of the soldier. He stood up with a sigh of relief.

"Food," he explained. "Sent by my father, Jesse. He has three sons in the army. This is our contribution to the war effort."

"Well just give it a bit more effort," said the soldier. "Carry that lot into the storage tent, sharpish. A soldier like me can't be wasting strength preparing lunches. Uh oh… here comes trouble."

The soldier made a sudden dash for the storage tent as a low growling from beyond the camp rose to a bloodcurdling howl. David ran after him and with the basket.

"Do you mind if I go and see the battle?" he asked, delightedly. But he didn't wait for an answer.

Instead, he raced off to find his brothers.

They were among the ranks, shouting the war cry. David pushed to the front, hoping to see the Philistine army marching forward to battle.

Oh. There was no approaching army. David found himself gazing open-mouthed at just one fighter towering over his shield bearer.

The sun glinted on the giant's bronze armour and his iron-tipped weapons.

18

David turned to ask what was going on, but his brothers simply weren't there any more.

"Come away with everyone," hissed another soldier. "That's Goliath. He's challenging us to one-on-one combat.

"You don't want to go volunteering for that job," he explained as he hustled David to safety. "King Saul may be promising a big reward, but you wouldn't live to claim it."

"Yes, I would!" came the reply. "I'd love to be part of the fighting. Who was that top-heavy metal-plated coward anyway? I could pick him off in no time."

David's eldest brother was not impressed when he heard his youngest brother boasting. "You cheeky brat!" he said. "You can't fight. You think this is like a game. Get back to your baa-lambs, will you?"

David shrugged and sauntered off. Brotherly insults – what did he care? Instead he began pestering anyone and everyone. Did he have to ask King Saul before he went to fight? Was it absolutely definite about the big reward? Could he, David, do the fight today as tomorrow was a bit of a problem with the stand-in shepherd who was minding the sheep?

In the end, King Saul heard what was going on.

"Bring the lad here," he

sighed. "I don't want to send someone who will lose the war for us."

David came and explained his plan. The servants exchanged sidelong glances.

"He has rather more exuberance than is customary when dealing with royals," they whispered.

Saul was already shaking his head. "You're just a boy," he said. "Goliath has been a fighter all his life."

"Your Majesty," replied David, suddenly remembering all his father had told him about showing respect to Those in Authority.

"I'm a shepherd boy. I've killed lions and I've killed bears.

"I believe I can beat Goliath because I believe in God and that God will help me."

Saul reflected for a moment. He had no other volunteers. The Philistines could change tactics and come and destroy his men any time.

"Take my armour," he announced gloomily. "And God be with you."

Gleefully David tried the royal armour. Then he flung it off.

"I'm not used to fighting like that," he said. "I'll do it my way." He set off outside.

"Watch this," he called cheerfully to his brothers, "and learn."

He walked down the hill, swinging his staff. At the stream he stopped to pick up five small pebbles.

He walked up the opposite hillside to where Goliath was waiting.

"Do you think I'm a dog," snarled the giant, "and you are going to beat me with your stick?"

"Loser," cried David. "You've put all your trust in lumps of metal. I've put my trust in God."

eurrghAARRGH

Goliath roared and lumbered forward. David sprinted nearer. He fitted a stone to his sling, whirled – and threw.

The stone hit. Goliath stumbled and fell heavily. His armour pinned him down. David ran forward, grabbed the giant's sword, and cut his head off.

THE PROPHET OF DOOM AND GLOOM

THE STORY OF JONAH

Jonah was a prophet – a man with the wisdom and courage to bring God's message to the world. At least, he was supposed to be.

THE SHIP'S CAPTAIN was surly.

"I sometimes take passengers," he told Jonah. "But passengers are a nuisance on a cargo ship. I have to charge a price that makes it worth my while. And Tarshish, where we're bound for, is a long, long way."

"Name your price," replied Jonah. "I feel drawn to the lands of the west."

The sailors watched as Jonah agreed a fare with the captain. "Why would anyone want to go to Tarshish or fun?" they muttered. "We're only going because of the pay."

"I spent some time in Nineveh, up north," sighed one. "Now that's the city for me. Fabulous buildings, great markets, and the best places to eat and drink anywhere."

Jonah had his reasons for choosing Tarshish. He got on board and the ship set sail. He watched the shore fade as they left the east behind. He watched the sun set in the west. Then he went below to sleep, delighted to be on his way.

"What? What? What's going on! Leave me alone." Jonah awoke in confusion.

"Get up, landlubber," the captain was shouting. "Can't you tell there's a storm? Come up and help save the ship! Pray to whatever god you worship!"

As Jonah stumbled onto the deck, a sailor passed him a bag. "Pick out the first thing you touch," he growled, Jonah did as he was told. The sailors gathered around, each taking an object from the bag. They showed what they had taken. It was a choosing game. Everyone was looking at Jonah.

"So," snarled the first mate. "It's our passenger we have to blame for this, is it?" snarled the first mate. "Your god is angry with you and that's why this storm is going to DROWN US ALL!"

Jonah held up his hands in terror. "I give in," he said. "I know

what I'm running away from. Throw me overboard, and then all will be well and the storm will stop."

"I'm sorry you've wasted your fare," whispered the captain, with surprising kindness, as he grabbed one of Jonah's arms.

"Quite alright," said Jonah. "Where I'm going, I won't have to worry about the cost of living ever again."

The first mate picked up one of Jonah's legs. Together the two sailors swung their passenger into the raging sea.

Down went Jonah: down, down, down.

Down, down, GLUB!

What was that? Why the sudden calm? Where was he? It was like… a cave… but warm… and slimy.

Jonah took a deep breath to steady himself. Just a moment. Hold that thought. He'd just taken a breath. HE WAS STILL BREATHING.

"O God," he prayed, "I don't really understand. I thought I was dying, but now I've still got a chance. Save me, please. I'll do anything – everything – I'll do that thing I was running away from. O God! Help!!!!!!"

The next thing Jonah knew, he was gasping in a tumble of surf and being grated on the sand. He was on a beach. Out to sea, a huge sea creature leaped and plunged. Its tail vanished beneath the waves.

Could he believe what he was seeing? Had God sent a sea creature to save him? Well, how else had he got here?

Jonah picked himself up. "Nineveh, here I come," he said. "I'm going to tell it like it is: how wicked you Ninevites are, and how

powerfully my God can act to DESTROY you all!"

So he went to the glittering city. He told the people that they must change their ways or face God's anger.

And the people of Nineveh, who had never paid any attention to God but instead to their fabulous buildings, their great markets, and the best food and drink available anywhere in the known world… well, they changed their ways. The king, the grown-ups, the children, the lot.

And God forgave them.

Jonah built himself a little hut overlooking Nineveh. In vain he waited for the city's destruction. No fire, no brimstone, not even a bad storm.

"God, I'm so angry," said Jonah. "I knew you'd do that. You always do."

He was boiling with rage. And with the sun. Was it hot!

Then, as if by a miracle, a seed sprouted. A plant grew. Its leaves spread over the hut and gave cool shade.

"What a blessing," exclaimed Jonah. "Praise be!"

In the night, a worm came and ate the stem of the plant. Jonah awoke to find the leaves limp and drooping.

"My poor, dear, plant!" he cried.

Quietly, God spoke. "Dear dear, Jonah. You care so much about your plant. Yet you did nothing to bring it into being.

"If you care so much about a plant, why shouldn't I care about the people of Nineveh, and all its animals: the living, breathing creatures that I have made?"

TAKING THE HEAT

THE STORY OF THE FIERY FURNACE

*Sometimes you just have to stand up for what you believe in. It may
not be easy, but you just have to take the heat.*

KING NEBUCHADNEZZAR OF Babylon smiled. It didn't really suit his face. It didn't really suit his character.

"I have to say I'm really rather pleased today," he said. Beside him, the servants sighed with relief. Life was difficult if King Nebuchadnezzar was even ever so slightly disgruntled.

"The golden statue," the king continued. "It's splendid.

The craftworkers did fret about making it so tall, but with my urging, they have succeeded. I knew I was right to insist."

"It was your excellent design," said the chief craftworker, and he bowed. The king's urging had been rather painful. He felt glad to have survived it.

King Nebuchadnezzar turned to survey the crowds. "I am pleased to see that my summons was obeyed," he said.

"Oh yes," said his chief messenger. "These high officials are your obedient servants. They all said how privileged they felt to be invited. Many arrived very early."

"Excellent," said King Nebuchadnezzar.

He raised his hand. At the sign a herald called for silence.

"People of all nations, races, and languages," he cried. "The ceremony will begin with a fanfare of trumpets.

"Then the band will begin to play. The music will swell to a glorious crescendo.

"At that moment, you are all to bow down. Worship at the feet of this astonishing, amazing, incredible, and utterly divine golden statue!

"But beware: anyone who does not obey will be punished – thrown into a blazing, fiery furnace. Their ashes will be trampled in the mud."

He glowered at the crowd. He saw only scared faces. Good; people had been listening. The herald lifted a trumpet to his lips.

Almost before the first note had sounded, the high officials were on their knees, their faces low to the ground.

The chief craftworker nudged the chief messenger. "Look, over there," he whispered. "I said they'd do that."

"Over there", three men were still standing.

The chief messenger performed the elaborate bow to show he wished to speak to the king without first being spoken to.

"Your Majesty, with regret," he said. "You put your trust in some of the captives from Judah. They are not worthy of your trust. Look: they are not bowing down."

King Nebuchadnezzar did not like to be told what to do. He turned very, very slowly to where the messenger was pointing. What he saw made him so angry his eyes bulged.

He spat an order. "Bring them here at once."

Servants rushed to obey. Within minutes, Shadrach, Meshach, and Abednego were being dragged to the king.

"Did you not hear the COMMAND?" Nebuchadnezzar demanded to know. "Do you not know the PUNISHMENT?"

The three young men stood tall. "We worship the God of our people, our God alone," they replied coolly. "We believe our God can save us from your punishment. But whatever happens, we would rather die than bow down to your statue – we think that's wrong."

King Nebuchadnezzar turned red with rage. He turned to the Foreman of Furnace. "Stoke the fire," he demanded. "Make it burn seven times hotter. Then tie up these traitors and hurl them in."

He watched the preparations with a cruel, crooked expression. He barely raised an eyebrow as the guards who marched the prisoners to their doom were themselves sucked into the flames.

Then something made him frown. He leaned forward to look more closely. He turned to the Foreman of Furnace and spoke in an angry whisper.

31

"You useless slave. I told you to tie the men tight! But I see them walking around, dancing."

He paused. Then he turned white with terror and clutched the foreman. "There is someone else in there! Look – can't you see, you fool? A heavenly being, a god."

He ran forward screaming: "Shadrach, Meshach, Abednego! Come out! COME OUT AT ONCE."

The three young men walked out of the furnace; they had no injuries from fire, angel encounters, nor even dancing. King Nebuchadnezzar swayed slightly with shock. His legs wobbled. Had the Carriers of the Royal Chair not been to hand, he would have collapsed in a rather unroyal way.

After a few moments he recovered enough to stand up.

"Everyone," he said, "listen. Hush. I have a declaration to make. Scribe – write this down, it's important.

"I hereby declare that there is no god like the god of Shadrach, Meshach, and Abednego. Their God has saved them from what I planned to be certain death.

"I declare that no one in the empire must ever – ever, ever – say anything bad about their God."

He thought for a moment. He was already feeling more like his old self. "And if anyone does," he roared as he rose to his feet, "they will be torn limb from limb!"

RICH MAN, POOR MAN

THE PARABLE OF DIVES AND LAZARUS

Jesus often told stories: parables. For some of his listeners they were just entertainment. But the stories had a deeper message: not necessarily a comfortable one.

THERE WAS ONCE a rich man who had everything money could buy. The clothes he wore, the food he ate, the mansion where he lived: everything he owned just oozed luxury.

Another word people used for the things he had was

33

"covetable". It meant they longed to have those things for themselves. The snag was that one of God's Ten Commandments named coveting as a serious no-no. Respectable people would pretend they weren't a bit jealous of all that wealth. That's easy enough to do if you can manage without the money.

But there was a poor man named Lazarus who really needed a handout. He never had proper food, nor was there any place he could call home. Being hungry, being cold, and sleeping rough ruined his health. He had dreadful sores all over his body. They oozed pus.

Every day the poor man would come and sit outside the rich man's door. All he dared hope for was that he could pick over the rubbish for something to eat. He had to take his chances with every stray mongrel that came sniffing around for the same scraps.

He'd managed to make friends with some of them, and sometimes the dogs would lick his sores.

One day, the poor man died. Holy angels gathered around to carry him to heaven. There he was invited to feast with Abraham, one of the great prophets of ancient times.

About the same time, the rich man died. No one can buy their way out of death, however wealthy they are. He went down, down, down to the shadows. Now it was his turn to suffer.

He looked up to heaven, and there he saw Lazarus having a totally blissful time.

"Father Abraham," he called. "Help! Please send Lazarus down with just a drop of water for me here. The heat is dreadful – I'm tormented with thirst."

Abraham looked down. "You had your share of good times," he replied. "And you didn't care a fig about Lazarus while he was having more than his share of bad times. Anyway, there is a great pit lying between where we are and where you are, and no one can cross it. Sorry."

"Oooh!" groaned the wealthy man. "Then there is no hope left for me.

"Let me just beg of you one kindness.

"Send Lazarus back to the place where my father still lives. He has five other sons who are also wealthy. Unless someone warns them, they too will come to this place of pain and suffering."

Abraham fixed the rich man with a steely gaze. "They know the rules," he said. "The Ten Commandments and all that. Not coveting stuff, being generous to those in need. The words of the prophets have given them all the warning anyone could expect."

"I know, I know," wailed the rich man. "But all that goody-goody religious stuff doesn't seem important in the hustle and bustle of everyday.

"Now, if someone were to come back from the dead – I'm thinking Lazarus – that would make them take notice."

Abraham shook his head. "If they won't believe a prophet, they won't believe anyone. Not even someone who comes back from the dead."

And that was the end of the conversation; the end of the story; the end of the rich man.

A Tax Collector in a Tree

The story of Zacchaeus

*What happens if you get branded a cheat? What can you do
to make people think well of you again?*

THE QUEUE TO the tax collector's booth snaked around the
marketplace. There were three reasons why it was so long.
First, it was the last day to pay taxes without being charged a fine.
Second, the local builder was having an argument with the tax

collector, Zacchaeus. We'll get to the third in a moment. Back to the argument.

"What do you mean, that's not the right money?" the builder demanded to know. "It's the same as I paid last year, and I've earned the same this year."

"I had to add in the late payment fine," said Zacchaeus, briskly.

"I'm not late," said the builder. "It may be the last in-time day to pay, but not a late day."

"The date given," said Zacchaeus smugly, "has been wrongly understood as the last in-time day. It is, in fact, the first late day."

"You lying cheat!" growled the builder. "You're overcharging and you know it. That's how you got your fancy house, isn't it? Awarded yourself a bonus for being the thievingest tax collector in the empire."

"Or I have to give you a term in prison," said Zacchaeus. "As you can see, the guards are here."

Zacchaeus clicked his fingers and two Roman soldiers marched over. The builder glared at them. Then he slammed some extra coins on the desk and stormed off.

"Every time!" he complained to the waiting queue. "Every time he thinks of a way to get his hands on more of our money than even the emperor demands."

The muttering from the queue was clear proof that they agreed with him.

Now, the third reason for there being so many people in the centre of Jericho was that Jesus was coming to town. Jesus was news: not so much for his preaching about God, though some were very taken with it, as for the miracles that everyone talked about. Could Jesus really make the blind see, the lame walk, the dead rise to life?

As the day wore on, people left the marketplace to line the route. Zacchaeus closed his booth and went to find a place to stand.

Oh dear. He couldn't see. That was the problem with being short. He tried to worm his way to the front.

"Ow!"

Someone planted an elbow in his face.

"Oh, silly me," said the builder. He planted himself firmly in Zacchaeus's way and stayed there. Wherever Zacchaeus wriggled, the builder was in front of him, and all around the crowds sniggered. Zacchaeus heard someone use the words "payback time".

There was a little extra jostling, and Zacchaeus found himself pushed up against one of the trees that lined the route.

It was then that Zacchaeus had an idea. A tree! Surely he still had the skills learned as a boy raiding other people's orchards. He could climb quite high and sit quite comfortably on a branch. It took no time at all. And look – THERE WAS JESUS!

There was Jesus indeed. Looking up at Zacchaeus. The preacher gave a wave. "Come down, Zacchaeus," he said. "I've heard about your lovely house. I want an invite!"

Zacchaeus hurried down. Not very elegantly, but coming down

was always tricky. Even trickier when you're being booed. But Zacchaeus didn't care too much about that, nor indeed about the grumbling in the crowd as he led Jesus through the market square. He'd never worried about what kind of people lived in the crumbling parts of town along the way. He was eager to reach the leafier outskirts where his mansion stood behind high walls.

The meal his servants prepared was excellent. Jesus was clearly someone who appreciated first-class food and top-notch wine. And he was a great storyteller – wit and wisdom all together. No wonder he was so popular.

Jesus' words – they had something about them. The ring of truth, maybe. Unforgettable certainly. Niggling even. Yes, niggling.

Zacchaeus later described the moment as like a lamp being lit in a dark room. He saw things clearly. And he didn't like what he saw.

Almost on impulse, he stood up. "From now on," he said, "I'm going to do things differently. I'm going to sell up and give half what I have to the poor. And if I've cheated anyone, I will pay back four times as much."

It was the servants who spread this unlikely news through the town and in the taverns. "Jesus was really pleased," they explained. "Said it was moments like this that made his work worthwhile."

"But we didn't get to see a miracle," said someone with a sigh.

The builder put down his drink on the tavern table. "I've worked out the repayment I'm due," he said. "Four times what he cheated me. That's a miracle."

LAW AND ORDER

THE STORY OF PAUL IN PHILIPPI

No one is above the law. Those who police it had better take care to keep it.

THERE WAS TROUBLE in Philippi. Big trouble. The jailer had a good view of the goings on from the prison window. Down in the main square, some kind of riot was starting up.

A short, stout man whom the jailer knew to be one of the Town Bigwigs was getting into a fluster and waving his arms around. No one was listening. In desperation he ran to the top of a flight of steps. "Hush!" he pleaded.

42

No one hushed. Little Mr Bigwig stood there opening and shutting his mouth like a fish.

Then armed guards arrived from the garrison, clattering their weapons. The crowd fell silent. There was another clatter as a market trader was knocked over into his stall of vegetables. A child giggled nervously.

By now a group of bigwigs had made their way to the safety of the steps. From the front of the crowd a man began to shout.

"I want these two scoundrels punished," he cried, indicating two men who were being trussed up with ropes. "They have put some kind of spell on one of my most valuable slaves.

"She used to tell fortunes, and I got a lot of business from her talents.

"Now they say they've healed her, and she's lost the gift. And I've lost my income. I WANT JUSTICE!"

"What's more," added the man's friend, "the troublemakers are Jews." The largely Roman crowd booed enthusiastically at that. The officials whispered among themselves. Then Little Mr Bigwig made an announcement.

"We have decided," he said, "that the accused should be whipped. They will be flogged right here, right now. Then they will be put in jail to await our further deliberations."

The guards seemed to have come prepared for the task. They beat the two men until their skin bled. The crowd jeered as they were carried away to where the jailer was waiting, jangling his keys.

He led the way to an inner room where he clamped both pairs

of legs into wooden blocks. Then greeted his new guests.

"Scum," he said.

"Paul actually," said one of the prisoners.

"And Silas," said the other.

"Shalom," they chorused. It was the Jewish greeting. "Peace."

"Right," said the jailer. "Let's have peace and quiet, shall we?"

He didn't think about them as he went back to his chair overlooking the square. He didn't care that they were in the dark

44

while he watched the sunset. He didn't wonder about whether or not they might like some water as he poured himself a nice end-of-day tipple.

He did think about them around about midnight, when the singing started. Hymns, he could tell that by the words. Now the other prisoners were starting to join in. He was going to get up right now and…

AAAARGH

The jailer found himself thrown onto the floor. The whole room shook. Every door in the building swung open. A shout of "FREEDOM!" rose up from the cells.

"Snakes alive!" muttered the jailer. "The prisoners are going to escape. I'll be crucified for falling down on the job. I'd rather die by my own sword!"

He pulled a steely blade from the scabbard that hung by his side.

"Stop. Calm down." It was Paul. "We're all here," he said. "No one's going to take advantage."

The jailer looked at him, his eyes round with fear. "What do I need to do?" he asked warily.

"To be saved?" asked Paul. "Listen to what I have to tell you. About someone called Jesus. We are followers of the way that he taught, and the message could change your life."

The jailer was suddenly eager to please this strange preacher who had come his way. He had a nagging worry that the earthquake that had cracked open the prison had been sent by the man's god. He sent a message for his wife to start getting a meal ready. He fetched water to clean up the men's wounds. He listened carefully to all they had to say.

Turning away from sins and leading a righteous life had not been high on his to-do list but it did seem like a good idea.

And now his wife was asking about where the weekly meetings of their group were. How to join. No doubt about that, then; they were both going for it: a fresh new start. It felt like good news.

The next morning, the guards came back with a message.

"Case dropped," they said. "Set Paul and Silas free."

"What fantastic news!" the jailer replied. Paul shook his head and wagged his finger at the guards.

"Oh no," he said. "We may be Jews but we are also Roman citizens, and someone had us whipped without a trial. That's punishable under Roman law. Maybe even a jail term. Go and tell Little Mr Bigwig and his friends that we don't go until they say sorry."

Paul and Silas got their apology. Oh yes.